The Mad Family Gets Their Mads Out

Fifty Things Your Family Can Say and Do to Express Anger Constructively

LYNNE NAMKA, ED. D.

ILLUSTRATED BY NANCY SARA

Talk, Trust and Feel Therapeutics

TUCSON, ARIZONA

Also by Lynne Namka
The Doormat Syndrome

Avoiding Relapse: Catching Your Inner Con
Both published by iuniverse.com and available directly through
www.iuniverse.com

How to Let Go of Your Mad Baggage*

Good Bye Ouchies and Grouchies, Hello Happy Feelings*

**Teaching Emotional Intelligence to Children: Fifty Fun
Activities for Families, Teachers and Therapists***

All published by **Talk, Trust and Feel Therapeutics**
5398 Golder Ranch Road
Tucson, AZ 85739

Published by
Talk. Trust and Feel Therapeutics
5398 Golder Ranch Road Tucson, Arizona 85739

Printed in the United States of America

Library of Congress Catalog Card Number 94-60804
ISBN 0-9642167-0-1

Dedication

Dedicated to all children and all of our Inner Children who learned the message of *"Don't talk, don't trust, don't feel,"* and subsequently go through life stuffing their feelings, resulting in submissiveness and/or anger.

Special thanks go to Renu Benepal and the teachers and children of the Sonora Desert Early Childhood Program and the Desert Hills Early Childhood Program.

I was mad.
I saw red! I roared fire!
I screamed and stormed.
But I was still mad!

I was so mad.
I blew my top and yelled, "I hate **you!** It's all your **fault!"**
I stomped my foot, ran to my room and slammed the door.
But I was still mad!
And I felt bad.

I was mad.

I was so mad that I had to hit something.

So I punched the wall.

I threw my toys across the room.

But I was still mad.

And besides my hand hurt.

And I felt really bad.

They grew bigger and bigger.
They grew bigger than I was!
I had the big, bad mads.
Those mads stuck around.
They wouldn't go away.

The madder I got, the more others got mad back at me.
The people in my family were mad too.
We were a mad, mad family.
And I felt sad.

My mom said to my dad, "We've got to do something about that boy."

"It seems as if he's mad all of the time.
He's just like you."

Then they got in a fight about whose fault it was.
Then I really felt bad.

Mom and dad took me to see a nice lady.
"It's a case of the mads coming out in the wrong way,"
said the lady.

She explained, "Everyone has mads. It's okay to get mad.
But mads get stuck and then they pop out and get you in
trouble."

"Here," she said, "Slip on this Mad Jacket."

I put it on.
I sagged under the weight.
It must have weighed ten tons.
This Mad Jacket was heavy. *Heavy!*

"Is that how you feel?" she asked.
"All weighted down?
Like there is a heavy weight on your shoulders?
You get upset because people are angry at your house."
"Is that how it is, heavy?"

I nodded.
Heavy. That's how it felt to be angry all of the time.

"You might feel like you are ready to blow up," said the lady.
"Do your jaws get tight and your stomach feels funny?
Are your fists curled up all of the time, ready to hit?"

Yow!
This lady knew about mads.

"Or maybe you go numb and try not to feel the anger?" she asked.

"Holding on to bad feelings is like canning worms.
You stuff those mad feelings into a can.
You push them way down.
Those cans of worms hide in your tummy.
The more you push down, the worse you feel.
Those cans get fuller and fuller.
Then they get too full and you blow up, yell or hit someone.
Then people get mad at you.
And you get more mads.
Is that right?"

I nodded again. That is how it was.
"Yuck!" I said, thinking of those cans of worms in my stomach.

The lady asked, "When your mom and dad fight, do you feel all scary inside?
Maybe you just stand there and listen-frozen and confused.
Maybe you try to get into the fight.
Later when the scared feelings go away, the angry ones come.
And then you go hit something. Right?

Boy was that lady right.
Grownups have mads too.
Big grownups have big mads.
My Mon and Dad have lots of mads.

"Well here is what you can do to take care of yourself" she said.
"Say to yourself 'Grownups fight. They make up.
It's a grownup problem. It's not my problem.
I'll make a good choice. I'll take care of myself.'"

She asked my parents, "Is it okay if he takes care of himself when you fight?
My parents smiled and agreed.

"This is a safe place to let the mads out."
The lady handed me a box of crayons.
"Draw some pictures when you feel bad inside."

So I drew my mads.
I made them big and dark and ugly.
"Yep, those are mads all right!" she said.
"Now let's pound the mads.
Put them in this clay."

So I pounded my mads into that clay.
I hit that clay hard.
The lady showed me how to make mad noises as I hammered
away.
I made big *maaaad* noises!

"Now let's play the mads out," she said.
"Here is a mad snake family.
The little snake has lots of mads that he needs to get out.
Show me."

I took that little snake and made it pounce on the big one.
The little snake grabbed the big one by the tail.
And swung it around, crashing it down on the floor.
Then I tied the big snake in knots and jumped up and down on it.

"That's sure a lot of mads," said the lady and she smiled.
"It's good to see those mads coming out in a safe place."

"We can't hurt people. People are not for hurting. You can learn to get the bad feelings out in safe ways.

Now check your tummy. Any more mads left?"
"Yep, I'm still mad," I announced.
"Then talk them out." she said.
"Talking is the best thing you can do when you're angry.
You can learn to tell people about your mads in a nice way.
Now tell me about your mads."

So I told her about how mad I was when...
    Mom said no cookies before dinner.
    The teacher scolded me for being noisy in a group.
    My friend Jenny hit me for no reason at all.
    Dad yelled at me for spilling my milk.
    Mom and dad were fighting.
    And I couldn't go out and play any old time I wanted to.
    I got a spanking for no reason at all —
        Well, almost no reason.

We practiced talking out the mads.

The lady showed me how to tell my mads.

She said I could say my mads out loud using a strong, firm voice.

She told me to remember to use my words when I was mad.

I chose the teddy bear for my teacher.

"I feel mad when you scold me for talking in class," I said.

The baby doll became my little brother.
"I feel mad when you knock my blocks down."

I pretended that the hippo was my father.
I felt kind of scared with my dad there watching me.
The lady nodded.

I took a deep breath and said, "I feel mad when you yell at me."
I looked at my father to see if he was angry.
But my dad just nodded too.

"You are learning to use your words," said the lady.
"It's okay to feel mad some of the time.
But holding onto angry feelings only makes you feel bad.
Hurting people by calling them names makes you more angry.
Using your words in a nice way chases those bad feelings
away."

"Check your body, it will tell you when your mads are coming
on. Then tell yourself to make a good choice and use your
words."

"Breathing helps you think better when you are angry." she said.
"You can blow those mads away by taking deep breaths."

"Here is what you say to yourself. It goes like this:

I feel mad-I breathe.
Feel mad-breathe.
Mad-breathe.
Mad-breathe."

"Do it with me," she said.
I thought of my angry feelings.
Then I remembered to breathe.
I blew out some of my mads.
I told myself to make a good choice.
"Now how do you feel?" asked the lady.
I checked my tummy.
There weren't any mads!
My fists…no mads there.
My brain…there were no mads anywhere! The mads were gone!

The lady said, "Now say 'When I talk my mads, they go away.'
When you say it, drop off the Mad Jacket," said the lady.

So I did. I said, "I can talk my mads away."
I dropped that heavy Mad Jacket on the floor.
No more mads. No more heaviness.
I felt light.
That felt good.

"The mads are gone for now" said the lady.
"They may come back.
They might sneak back in when you don't get your way.
Or when Mom or dad says no.
Or if someone hurts you or takes away your toys.
That's just the way mads are."

"But now you know how to take care of them.
Remember to check your feelings.
Breathe. Blow out your mads.
Talk them out. Then you can feel good about yourself."

She said to my mom and dad, "He's going to get his mads out nicely now. Can you let him do it?
He will need some reminders."
Mom and dad nodded.

"You can help him by getting your mads out too. You can be a family that lets its anger out in ways that don't hurt people.
You can become a "speak your feelings kind of family."

Mom and Dad talked about their own mads with the lady.
I made the little snake beat up the grownup snake again, just
in case...

"Remember every one gets angry," said the lady.
"It's okay to get angry.
But stop and think when you do.
Make good choices about how you let the anger out.
Talk your feelings. Tell someone how you feel.
Choose a safe person who will listen to you.
Use your words in ways that do not hurt others or yourself."

"You will have to remind each other about what you've
learned," said the lady.
Mom and Dad smiled at each other.
I grinned back.
We agreed to tell each other "Use your words!"

The lady looked sad. "In some families the parents stay mad,"
she said. "Then all a boy or girl can do is remember to make a
good choice and take care of themselves. They can't wait for
their parents to get it."

The next day my friend Jenny bumped into me.
Accidentally, kinda, sorta on purpose.
I felt my jaws and my stomach get tight.
I took a deep breath in and out.
I stopped and thought.
Then I told my friend, "I feel mad when you bump me!"
"Sorry," said Jenny.
My mads got smaller.

When Mom said I had to go to bed I started to get steamed.
I didn't want to go to bed.
"Make a good choice," she said. "Breathe and get your control.
Use your words."

So I did. I took deep breaths and got my control. I
remembered my words.

I told my Mom, "I'm getting angry, will you listen to
my words?"
My Mom nodded.
I still had to go to bed, but it helped to talk about it.
My mads got even smaller.

I told my Dad, "I feel mad when you won't play."
"Yep, that's the way it is," said my Dad.
"I can't play right now.
Maybe we can play later."
My mads got smaller and smaller.

One day Mom and Dad were fighting.
My stomach started to hurt and I felt bad.
I decided to leave and take care of myself.
As I left, I said, "Mom, use your words.
Tell Dad you are mad."
They looked surprised.
Then they laughed.

Wow! I had discovered something!
You can let your mads out when you use your words!

The skyscraper I built fell over.
I said to myself, "I feel mad when I can't make things go right.
Sometimes things don't go the way I want."
Then I remembered. It's okay to feel mad.
It's what I do with my angry feelings that counts.
I can be angry at myself or I can let go of my mad!
I decided to breathe and try again. Why get mad at myself?

Sometimes the other person didn't like what I said.
When my big sister called me names I said,
"I feel mad when you call me names.
I am not stupid. Don't call me that ugly name."

"Bug off," said my sister.
It felt good anyway because I let my mad out.

When another kid tried to ram my bike, I said,
"I feel mad when you hit my bike. Stop it."
He gave me a mean look and called me a name.
He curled up his fists, but he didn't hit me.
He rode away.

I felt good because I had told him how I felt.
I had let that mad out.

Yeah!

The more I told my mads, the smaller they got!

I got pretty good at it.

Mom and Dad and my big sister started talking their mads too.

We became a "speak your feelings" family!

No more seeing red and roaring fire.

No more going numb and stuffing my feelings!

No more exploding!

No more hitting the wall!

No more screaming "It's all your fault!"

No more yelling "I hate you!"

Well, things are starting to be different at my house now. I just tell my mads in a nice way. I use my words.

Now I feel...*happy!*

Rules For Getting Your Mads Out

✓ Check your tummy, jaws and your fists. See if the mads are coming.

✓ Breathe! Blow your mad out.

✓ Get your control. Feel good about getting your control.

✓ Stop and think; make a good choice.

✓ People are not to be hurt with your hands, feet or voice. You can't hurt people just because you are mad.

✓ Remember to use your firm words, not your fists.

✓ Use a strong voice and talk your mads out. Say "I feel mad when you_____."

✓ Sometimes you need to take a time out to get your control back.

✓ Take yourself off to a safe place and talk to yourself.

✓ Pat yourself on the back for getting your mad out nicely.

Things To Do Later
If The Mads Are Still There

✓ Remember, mads don't have to stay inside you. Talk to someone who can help you sort out the feelings that make you feel bad.

✓ Draw lots of pictures about what makes you angry. Make big, colorful angry drawings. Make mad noises when you draw. **Big, mad noises!**

✓ Put your pictures in the freezer to cool off those mads. Or let your refrigerator hold pictures of your mads.

✓ Pound on clay or on pillows. Scream and yell and pull those mads out of your stomach. Let those mads run down your fists and into the pillow.

✓ Go out in the back yard and dig a hole. (Or just pretend to dig in your living room.) Pull all those mads up and out of you and put them down in the hole. Then cover them up with dirt and jump up and down, stomping on the mads.

✓ Put your mads in soap bubbles and blow them away. Watch those feelings float up to the sun and poor! Act out the story of your mads with dolls, stuffed animals or plastic dinosaurs.

✓ Get permission to tear up an old magazine. Rip each page out, one by one as you make "big mad noises." Then throw those mad feelings away by putting all the pages in the trash.

✓ Get permission to put your anger in a raw egg. Write the name of the person you are mad at on an egg. Go to a wide open space and pull up all your mads to put in the egg. Throw your mads as far as you can and yell and scream..... *"Aaaaagh!"*

Things To Do If Someone Bigger Starts To Hurt You

✓ Leave. Don't stay. Take care of yourself.

✓ If the person is bigger than you, get away from him or her. Go to a safe place and take care of yourself. Find a place where you feel safe. Or run to some adult you trust or to your neighbor's house.

✓ Find some safe people to talk to. If the first person does not listen, find someone else.

✓ Remember kids should not be hurt. Not even parents are supposed to hurt little kids. Keep talking until you find someone to help you.

✓ If you or other people in your family are being hurt badly, call 911 and ask for help.

✓ If someone is touching you in ways that you do not like, call the Child Abuse Hot Line at 1-800-422-4453 (1-800-4-A-CHILD®)

Parents Get Mad Too!

Things to do instead of blowing your top and yelling at your kid

✓ Remember, anger as an emotion is normal human behavior. As a response, you have choices. Choose from the productive expressions of anger. Tell yourself... "It's OK to be angry. I choose to use my anger constructively." Anger can be a signal that something in your life needs changing. When your personal resources are exhausted, you are more likely to be angry. Plan alternative fun things for your child to do when you are fatigued or ill.

✓ Check your own stomach, fists, and jaw. Observe how your body starts to tense up and react automatically when you feel threat. Know when you are mad! Analyze your own patterns of responding to anger; know what your typical anger response is. Watch yourself as the heat starts to rise. Observing yourself may help break into your regular anger response. Break into your regular response pattern. Remember to breathe.

✓ Bite your tongue when the angry words start to arise. Gently, of course, to remind yourself to inhibit your angry verbal or striking-out response.

✓ Breathe deeply, then state your anger in a firm voice, "I feel angry, when you _____." Make this formula a habit in your family by your using it often. If you have problems saying it, practice on the dog or the mirror at first.

✓ Distract yourself for a short time before going into problem solving by:
  o Reciting the days of the week, months of the year or counting to ten in a foreign language.
  o Phone Dial a Joke, The Weather, the Daily Prayer or Time.
  o Take a walk or weed the garden.
  o Displace your anger by cleaning the house. Vacuum while you cool down.
  o Do a self-soothing exercise. Massage your arms and neck. Hug yourself. Take a warm bath. Smell a flower. Pet an animal. Hug a Teddy bear. As the National Committee for Prevention of Child Abuse says, "Take time out. Don't take it out on your kid!" Know it's okay to be angry.
✓ Bypass a negative anger reaction by going directly into problem solving. Don't try to fix blame. Determine what is needed to correct the situation. Contribute to the solution, not the problem.
✓ Call Parents Anonymous or a sympathetic friend. Make sure your child realizes you are reaching out for help in anger reduction not calling someone to blame him or her.
✓ If you continue to get angry at your child, seek professional help or take a parent training group. Whatever the cost, it is a bargain in providing stress reduction in your household. Short term therapy often offers techniques to insure good mental health for you and your child. The amount of money and time you use in learning practical tools of communication and discipline are an investment in your child's future.

Things For Parents To Say
To Ward Off A Mad Attack

✓ "Stop and think. Make a good choice."

✓ "Remember to breathe when your tummy gets tight. Breath. Let's breathe together."

✓ "Use your words, not your fists. People are not for hurting."

✓ "You can do it. I know you can get your mads under control."

✓ "I understand, right now you are feeling mad. Still, you can't hurt people, things or yourself."

✓ "You are the kind of kid who can take care of his own bad feelings."

✓ "Go to a safe place and draw out your mads."

✓ "You have a choice: Talk out your feelings or go to time out and get your mads under control."

✓ "Well, I'm feeling mad right now myself. I'm going to go cool off, and then we'll talk."

✓ "I know how you feel. Sometimes I get mad myself. Then I tell myself, "Its OK to be mad if you are nice about it.""

✓ "Thanks for sharing your angry feelings. Good choice in using your words!"

✓ "We are learning to be a 'Speak your feelings' kind of family. No more 'Mad Family' for us."

✓ "I believe in you. Sometimes it's tough, isn't it?"

✓ "You are one terrific kid!"